FROM SHADOWS and SYMBOLS to the TRUTH

Cor ad Cor loquitur

MARYGROVE COLLEGE
EX LIBRIS

APPROACH
TO
CALVARY

TO NICOLAS

*for whom the stations of the cross
have a special meaning*

APPROACH TO CALVARY

Dom HUBERT van ZELLER

SHEED AND WARD • New York

Contents

Illustrations

Preface

IN CASE THE READER should be misled by the illustrations, it might be as well to point out that this is not so much a book of devotion—a series of separate meditations on the Way of the Cross—as an essay on the subject of suffering in general. It can serve as a book of devotion as well—indeed its arrangement according to the fourteen stations has this secondary use in mind—but the primary purpose is to treat of problems connected with pain as a whole: why there has to be pain, how it justifies itself, what we are expected to do about it. Since the answer to all this is to be found in the Passion, it seemed suitable to relate particular aspects of human suffering to particular incidents of Christ's experience. The method has not everywhere been closely followed, but for the most part the questions which puzzle people with regard to suffering will be examined in the light of one or other station. In this connection it is worth noting that when the *Via Crucis* was first introduced, the faithful began with the Resurrection and worked backwards towards the Condemnation. Thus to the Christian of the fourteenth century the whole business of suffering was seen to take its cue from the mystery which frees from suffering. This is highly significant. Suffering, ours as well as Christ's, is to be understood in terms of its sequel. The clearer our vision of suffering's consequence, the truer our appreciation of suffering's cause.

To Dom Denis Agius and Mr. Kevin Tierney, who took the photographs, the deepest gratitude is here expressed.

APPROACH
TO
CALVARY

I: JESUS IS CONDEMNED BY PILATE

1

Condemnation

GOD DOES NOT condemn man to suffering; man condemns himself to suffering. God tells man what is needed
for happiness, and in refusing God's terms man condemns
himself to unhappiness. This happened in the beginning,
when Adam turned down the happiness which was his for
the taking, and it has happened ever since, when the sons
of Adam turn down the conditions on which happiness
may be enjoyed. If there is a difference between Adam's
case and ours, it is that the conditions are more explicitly
formulated now than they were then. Christ has told us the
secret of his happiness in the Father. The only happiness
which is proof against suffering is the happiness which
Christ came on earth to bring. Suffering is powerless to
extinguish the happiness which is conditioned by faith and
hope. Why? Because faith and hope are evidence of the

love which accepts the essential condition of being obedient to God's will. Original sin condemns man to suffering; actual sin condemns man to suffering; mistaking pleasure for happiness condemns man to suffering. If man thinks he can make better rules for happiness than those laid down by God, he must bear the consequences of his arrogance: he must bear the weight of suffering.

In the choice between the peace which God guarantees—a peace which spells happiness even in this life, let alone the peace which spells happiness in the next—and that which the world promises, man is fatally inclined to grab at what is offered in temporal currency. The world does not always follow up its promises, and even on the rare occasions when it does the peace which it provides is an illusory affair. A happiness which is immediately appreciable, which supplies an escape or serves as a compensation, will turn out to be a wasting asset: we shall want more and more of it, we shall be unable to do without its satisfactions, we shall come to look in every possible direction for something which will assure us of its possession. And even then, precisely because we are being greedy about it, it will elude us.

God, unlike the world, invariably fulfils his guarantee. But such is the blindness of man—a blindness brought about by staring at material objects seen out of focus—that often the fulfilment is not valued for what it is. The happiness is there, waiting for us, but we are too busy with the pretences of happiness to notice it. Lacking the happiness which we are meant to have, we go on being unhappy in the happiness which we are not meant to have. Thinking ourselves to be always on the verge of discovering what we want, we anticipate the decrees of God. "This is going to be satisfying at last," we say, concentrating on the satisfaction of the moment, "so I can call this beatitude and not worry about any other." Then the beatitude fades, and we find ourselves back at worrying about another. If we looked single-mindedly at the happiness which God holds out to us—the happiness which is not an end in itself but goes along with seeking first his kingdom—we would not have to worry about any other. We would be happy without anxiety. Such is peace. Only God can give this; the world can not. Apart from it, all happiness is ephemeral—at the mercy of either fear, remorse, doubt, exhaustion, or anticlimax. If man will not accept security in God, then he condemns himself to insecurity. God does not condemn him; he condemns himself.

While God does not condemn man to suffering, neither does man condemn God: Christ suffered because he chose to, not because Pilate chose suffering for him. Pilate had no power but that which was given him by the Father. Christ by his own will laid down his life; he was not bound to obey Pilate. At any moment during the trial he could have defied his judge and escaped suffering. He was bound only to obey the Father; and the Father's will was his own. In becoming obedient unto death, even to the death of the cross, Christ was conforming to his own plan. For the perfection of this plan, devised in the wisdom of the divine mind, it was necessary that there should be a human plan as well. Indeed there were other plans besides Pilate's—all combining to form a pattern in which Christ's obedience to the Father could be perfectly realized. There was Judas's plan and there was Herod's; there was the plan of Caiphas; there was the plan of the priests and council. All these were so many sub-plots in the drama of atonement as conceived in the mind of God. They were the outward means only— any one of which could have been dispensed with had Christ so chosen. But Christ decided to dispense with none of them. As each contributing factor came one after another to be fitted in to the scheme of atonement for man's sin, so Christ welcomed it. Suffering was not forced upon him; he chose it.

Just as Christ is representative, coming before the Father and before man as the second Adam, so Pilate is also representative, standing for the human race in its weakness. Christ, in the perfect fulfilment of his mission, not only makes reparation for sin but proposes the living model for redeemed humanity. Pilate, in the misuse of his authority, not only piles up personal guilt but becomes the living symbol of human falsehood. Christ, when he "dispossessed himself, and took the nature of a slave, fashioned in the likeness of men, and presenting himself to us in human form" (Phil. 2, 7), gave to man an example of perfect mastery; Pilate, when he thought to possess himself in human dignity by the employment of an evasive tactic, became an example of mental slavery. Where Christ took upon himself the guilt of mankind, Pilate tried to excuse himself from blame by retreating behind a symbolical gesture. Where Christ chose the way of suffering which led to his ultimate triumph over suffering, Pilate thought to get out of suffering's way and found himself ultimately beaten by it. Even if Christ, by his words and acts, had not taught us how to approach the question of suffering, we should have been able to learn it from the behaviour of Pilate.

If we cannot hide from suffering, at least let us not excuse ourselves when we try to. If we cannot, with Christ, choose the cross, at least let us not wash our hands of it. Its implication is there, whether we face it or not, and to deny its practical application in our lives is to deny one of the essential aspects of the Passion. To try, as Pilate did, to take the easy way out is folly; it is also unworthy of those who walk in the way of Christ. One of the greatest glories of the Christian is that his sufferings and Christ's are bound up together. What more encouraging consolation can there be in times of upset and sadness than the possession of a share in the Passion? It is this knowledge that can turn a human sorrow into the highest supernatural sacrifice.

The call of the Passion is the call, precisely, to sacrifice, and much of our religious response must depend (as will further appear in the next section) upon the attitude which we bring to the Christian ideal of self-surrender. Here, as always in the affairs of religion, it is a matter of the will. Christ willed to lay down his life for man, and the sacrifice of Calvary was the result. His was the perfect immolation, voluntary and deliberate, which invited at the same time a corresponding act on the part of those who were to follow him as Christians. Had the crucifixion been imposed upon him against his will, there would have been a slaying only and not a sacrifice. Since the idea of sacrifice assumes the consent of the one sacrificing, the lesson of Calvary is something more subtle than the compulsory suffering which his enemies thought to be inflicting upon our Lord. The lesson of Calvary supposes a voluntary oblation of the victim as well as its destruction. It supposes further the summons to compassionate co-operation among the members of Christ's mystical body. This is, then, our approach to Calvary: we come bearing our own crosses, all men together, as fellow victims and co-sufferers with Christ.

II: JESUS RECEIVES THE CROSS

2

Acceptance

Suffering, left to itself, does not necessarily purify the soul. There is no guarantee that the sufferer is a better man than the non-sufferer. In some people the effect of suffering is seen to embitter and harden. Nor does God prefer to see us suffering rather than not suffering. Why, then, in the Christian concept is so much made of suffering? Would it not be healthier to concentrate on the enjoyment of life, and as far as possible to avoid the thought of suffering? Might not this preoccupation with the sorrows of human existence actually *attract* suffering—and so make the problem of living even harder than it is meant to be?

Certainly a case can be made out for attending to happiness in preference to unhappiness. God himself exists in bliss and not in misery. The blessed in heaven are enjoying their state without the least scruple. Christ came on earth to the accompaniment of joy, grew to manhood in the joy of charity which surrounded him, told his disciples that in him they might find a more abundant joy than they had ever known. The prophets preached the triumph of happiness which might be expected, even in this life, by those who were faithful to God's word; the psalmist is forever exalting the joyful praising of God's name; the saints of the Church are at one in revealing the note of joy in their lives. And on the negative side it is the absence of joy—still more, of course, the suppression of joy—which renders suspect a particular interpretation of sanctity. But this is not quite the point at issue.

The point here is not which is the better to develop, joy or sorrow, but how to take up the cross. Had Christ spoken of joy only, and not of suffering, there would be no problem. All we would have had to do would have been to perfect our attitude towards happiness. But he particularly did not say, "If any man be my disciple, let him take up his joy and follow me": the test of discipleship was to lie in the cross. So when the cross was actually placed upon his shoulders, Christ was concerned with teaching us the terms of a suffering discipleship. From our point of view the question which at that moment needed answering was not how to direct the feeling of joy but how to meet the circumstance of pain. The manner of his acceptance gives us the lead which we are looking for. He accepted the cross as a pain, but he accepted it with joy.

So it is that in the Christian understanding, as fashioned by Christ himself, joy and pain are not exclusive but compatible. Indeed we come to know joy through suffering and suffering through joy. The deeper the one, the truer the other. In itself, suffering is an evil: it is a negation of some particular good. Happiness, on the other hand, is something positive: it is a good towards which we have a right-ordered appetite. But once given the Passion, suffering *becomes* a good. A new element has entered in, turning the negation into an affirmation: suffering becomes a positive statement, proclaiming service, praise, union, love. The cross may be a stumbling-block to the Jews and to the Gentiles foolishness, but to us it is the appropriate expression of discipleship. In the alchemy of faith the bad is transformed into good, the debt becomes the gift, the stumbling-block is seen as the stepping-stone.

It is one thing to accept the doctrine and another to accept the fact. But it is the fact of the cross in our lives which will qualify our response to Christ. Our generosity is measured not by notional assents but by practical acts: how nearly do we approximate, in the trials by which we are tested, to the attitude of Christ when he received "the instrument with which he was to redeem the world"? Our

ideal is the mind of Christ, and we know that Christ welcomed the cross with love—with love for the Father's will
in allowing it, for his persecutors who imposed it, for us
who would benefit by it. Love gave meaning to the whole
thing. It was love which made the atonement adequate, the
obedience pleasing, the example inviting, and the actual
agony bearable. Dare we say that we endure with love the
crosses that are sent to us? No, of course we dare not say this,
but for our encouragement we should know that the motive
of love is at the top of the ladder and cannot always be
found at the bottom. From the lower dispositions we mount
to the higher, conscious always that it is Christ who goes before us bearing his own cross and that all we have to do is
to keep directing our steps after him.

Thus a man may, without offending against his Christian spirit, accept his cross because he has to. He feels no
love, he would escape it if he could, he plans to rid himself
of it at the earliest moment. Nevertheless, provided he receives the cross as coming from the will of God, he bears his
cross with Christ and his submission is accordingly pleasing to God. Higher up the scale is the man who wants
positively to please God in his suffering but who finds himself unequal to suffering's challenge. He has love as his motive, but it is a frustrated love: his weakness is too strong for
him, and his strength too weak. In this case, as in the other,

22

there is a certain resentment which prevents the response from being all it might be. Finally there is the man who walks towards the cross, and receives it with open arms. Although he may not know what he is in for, he is making as complete a sacrifice as he can; he trusts that God will give him the grace to carry his good intention to its conclusion. This is pure love, this is being one with Christ in his cross-bearing, this is the total surrender which verifies Christ's words about being lifted up and drawing all things to himself.

If all grace is received according to the disposition of the recipient, the particular grace of the cross must depend upon the degree of generosity with which the soul is prepared to meet it. If we open our hearts an inch we benefit an inch; if we open our hearts to full capacity, the cross has its unrestricted way with us and we become saints. An infant and an athlete may be given the same food, but where the infant will be quickly satisfied the athlete will clamour for more. The cross is the same because it is Christ's; it is we who differ. But there is nothing to say that the infant cannot grow into the athlete, that the shrinking cross-bearer cannot grow into a willing one. The whole thing depends upon grasping the principle of sacrifice, and allowing God's grace to draw all things in us to himself.

It was sacrifice which made the whole difference between Cain and Abel, between Saul and David, between the good and the bad thief. If sacrifice was an essential element in the religion of the Old Law, it is no less an essential element in that of the New. Our religious response would be meaningless without it. Every day reminding us of this, we have Christ's sacrifice reproduced for us in the Mass. If we do not learn from the Mass how to approach Calvary, we are not likely to learn it from this book. By the Mass, far more than by books, sermons, and good advice given to us by our friends, we are moved to offer our sufferings in union with those of Christ. The Holy Eucharist invites to identification not only with Christ in his sacramental body but with Christ in his sacrificial act. We see that the Mass is offered by Christ, priest and victim; we realize that we have a share in Christ's atoning prayer; we are drawn to participate actively in Christ's cross-bearing and death.

Thus it is in the Mass that our obligation to take part in the redemption of the world is brought home to us. The redeeming sacrifice is open to us, eliciting from us an oblation in the terms under which Christ lived out his whole life and which revealed itself finally in his acceptance of the cross at the hands of the Roman soldiers. Together with the still unconsecrated host we are on the paten; together with Christ in Pilate's courtyard we are waiting for whatever cross is fashioning. Worthless material of ourselves, we are caught

24

up into the infinite perfection of Christ. Our sufferings are nothing, but they are made into something by his. In virtue of our life in Christ—in virtue particularly of our eucharistic participation—we are made one victim with him in reparation for sin.

III: JESUS FALLS THE FIRST TIME

3

Failure

IT IS SIGNIFICANT that the prophet who laments that
God has "shut up my ways with square stones; he has
turned my paths upside down" is the same who speaks of
the Lord as "thinking thoughts of peace, and not of affliction" (Lam. 3, 9; Jer. 29, 11). It is significant that the
prophet who says "thou shalt be brought down, thou shalt
speak out of the earth" is the same who proclaims of God
that "the bruised reed he shall not break, and the smoking
flax he shall not quench" (Is. 29, 4; 42, 3). The implication
is clear: there is to be frustration, but the frustration will be
of a kind that can be explained by love, and which will
therefore not destroy but perfect. One might go one step
further and claim that without failure, the soul's experience
of love is incomplete. It is the story of Job: crushing reverses,
discouragement bordering on despair, the dawn of a new

hope and the birth of a new life. It is the theme-paradox of the New Testament: the seed dying that it may live, the folly of the cross being wiser than the wisdom of men, the weak things being chosen to overcome the strong, power being made perfect in infirmity, the finality of the Crucifixion preparing for the glory of the Resurrection. The doctrine could not be stated in starker terms: if we want to save our lives, we must lose them. In order to succeed we must fail.

It is possible to know Christ as the perfect model, as the leader, as the moral and spiritual teacher, but not to know him as one who, to outward appearances, was a failure. In the eyes of the world his mission, as it was seen at the time, came to nothing. Even in the eyes of his friends, as they saw him led away to death, the gospel hope which he had preached had let them down. If the agony in the garden was the sign of his defeat to his disciples, the first fall on the way to Calvary was the sign of his defeat to the outside world. Both to his own in private and to the others in public Christ willed to appear as a failure. It was his desire that all should imagine him to be without further resources, should think that he did not know what to do next. When a man falls to the ground it means that his strength has given out; the strain has been more than he was able to bear, and he is forced to show his weakness. For Christ to have endured the scourging was a sign of strength—was perhaps grounds for believing that he might yet surmount his difficulties and outmatch his enemies—but to have been seen falling was the sign that he was done for, that he had given in. Like the rest of men he was weak after all, and there were limits beyond which even he could not go. So it must have seemed to those who watched.

Thus if we are to resemble Christ we should expect to resemble him in failure. Failure is not our punishment but our privilege. We are never nearer to Christ than when we are beaten by the weight of life. It is when we are flattened and helpless that we can trust not in our power any more but in the power of God. When I am weak, then am I strong —because at last I can draw upon the source of strength which is God. God expresses himself in the helplessness of man: it is the Father's prerogative to come to the rescue of his children. If failure had no other value than that of making us childlike it would justify itself, but in fact its good effects can be seen in every aspect of the spiritual life. It teaches humility, compassion, and the need for perseverance, hope, faith, and a spirit of penance. Failure opens the door to the graces which follow upon the nights of the soul. The nights of the soul are, in fact, little else than an awareness of failure.

It is only when we have failed, uniting our frustrations

with the frustrations of Christ, that we come to see the over-all pattern of the gospel. The sermon on the mount is at last felt to be the only possible answer to the problems of man. The cross not only reconcilable but right—necessary and right. The Passion, because it is life, is a matter of fall-ing and being dragged up again. Our own story and Christ's are seen to have this unexpected affinity of weakness and re-newal, repeated until the final revelation of grace.

And in the meantime? What do we make of our falls, of the occasions when we are blocked, of the enterprises which held such promise but which have come to nothing? Even those collapses for which we are manifestly to blame—even our sins—can be turned to good account. There is noth-ing so bad that it cannot be taken up by grace and made into a potential good. If the knowledge of our moral failures can become material for compunction, dependence upon God, charity towards those who have been tempted and who have fallen in the same way, then certainly the frustrations to which we are liable in the unfolding of events must readily admit of supernaturalization.

Judged materially, the evils which Aeneas met with at the mouth of hell were daunting utterly. Sadness in old age, dire poverty, sickness and strife: these things spelled defeat at the hands of time and corrupting nature. These things, because they cannot be surmounted by human power, are witness to man's failure. Faced with these things man feels frustrated. But this is precisely where the Christian solution comes in. Christ proposes a life lived in a new dimension, a life of grace and faith. Given this life in Christ, the soul is proof against the frustrations of human life. The flaws which inevitably attend a created order which has known original sin no longer have the power to daunt utterly: they are judged materially no longer. When supernatural values are substituted for earthly values, a complete reversal takes place and the things which menaced before are now so many evidences of God's loving providence.

If God's kingdom were of this world, we would have reason to feel defeated at the reverses which we meet with in life. But because his kingdom is not of this world, and because we share the life which he lives in his own kingdom, we have no reason to feel defeated. He was destroyed by his persecutors, but he was not defeated. The burning bush of Moses' vision crackled in the flames but was not consumed. We die daily, but we go on living. With Christ we are nailed to the cross, with Christ we meet death, with Christ we go on rising again.

What, for the would-be follower of Christ, can be the alternative? Either he takes the way of the world or the way of faith. The worldling, from his last line of defence and when faced with capitulation, can draw no comfort from

31

the act of faith. He has no faith. The best he can do is to bow to the inevitable with a stoic grace. But even here he is surrendering to the material circumstance. Still more is he surrendering to the material circumstance if he thrashes out blindly in his desperation, if he attributes his misfortune to sheer bad luck, if he complains of his wasted talents and indulges in self-pity. Already before the end he has surrendered; he knows he has no reserves. But the man of faith *has* reserves; he surrenders to nothing but the will of God. His desire is united to the desire which was in the mind of Christ when he fell on the road to Calvary. His failure is Christ's failure, the waste of his talents is the waste of Christ's. There is no question here of desperation, panic, self-pity, rebellion; no talk of accident or bad luck.

So it is that the Christian solution is found to solve only when it is applied in its completeness. Take away any part of it and you find anomalies and contradictions; you find that it does not work. In the most glaring way this is seen to be true when you subtract from the Christian obligation the duty of forgiveness or the duty of mutual trust. It is because these gospel principles have never been acted upon in world affairs that there has never existed even the possibility of lasting and universal peace. Take away the part of the gospel which has to do with failure, and you get—again, but not so obviously—an incomplete response. There is no way round it: if we would be perfect in Christ, we must fail with Christ. Nothing succeeds like Christian failure.

IV: JESUS MEETS HIS MOTHER

4

Compassion

THE ACT OF COMPASSION is, whatever the manner of its expression, primarily an interior one. It may show itself in any one of the corporal works of mercy, but before it brings the particular kind of relief which the situation demands it has to exist in the mind. Otherwise the acts might well be acts of vainglory. So much does it reside in the mind rather than in the performance that sometimes compassion does not have to show itself outwardly at all. It is simply there— waiting. The mere possession of it brings sympathy. It is at the ready, wanting to help in any way at all or in no way at all. In other words, compassion is not just an exhibition of pity; it is a virtue in the strict sense of being a habit. Compassion is co-suffering: constant willingness to share in the sufferings of others. It is yielding to another's cross as though it were one's own. It is *making* that other cross one's own.

Works of compassion are a sign that the virtue is possessed; they are not themselves the virtue. If by tossing him a coin I commiserate a poor man—truly co-miserating in his distress—I show that I possess at least enough of the love of God to see in him an object of charity. Thus the love of God has to be present before the coin is tossed; the coin is the outward expression of the inward activity. What is all this leading up to? It is meant to point to the conclusion that had Mary never brought outward relief to Christ's sacred humanity, she would still be Mother of Divine Compassion.

But because love does not remain inoperative, Mary's love must in fact have brought relief to Christ in his sufferings. Tradition gives us nothing more about the meeting between Christ and his mother on the way to Calvary than the fact that they saw one another. What passed between them we do not know, but if words did not it makes no difference. Christ was suffering, and Mary was suffering with him. Both knew this, and in the joint knowledge lay mutual compassion.

Accordingly perfect love, as found in Christ and his mother, supposes perfect compassion. The presence of love assumes compassion just as the absence of love disproves it. The saints could enter sincerely into the trials of others not because they had themselves always experienced such trials but because they loved God. Their love of God made them *see*. They saw into the sufferings of others and immediately wanted to share the pain which they saw there. "Bear the burden of one another's failings [or just "bear ye one another's burdens"]; then you will be fulfilling the law of Christ" (Gal. 6, 2). The law of Christ is the law of charity, and charity inevitably makes us compassionate. It is because charity gives us insight that we can take so much off the shoulders of others: our mere understanding, which is itself a gift of the Holy Ghost and an aspect of charity, lessens the weight.

Without the insight and direction which charity gives, the emotion may go by the name of compassion, but it cannot be accounted for truly supernatural virtue. The sympathy may be heroic—just philanthropy may be heroic: "if I should distribute all my goods to feed the poor" (1 Cor. 13, 3)—but if it hath not charity it profiteth nothing. If the inward activity of love were not the qualifying factor—a love which has God as its primary object—then the compassion of Mary would have to yield place to the emotion which has moved other mothers to acts of love for their sons. Was Agar's pity for her child, because so intensely expressed, more noble than the compassion of Mary? (Gen. 21, 16). Did Respha, because her lamentation was accompanied by such privation, mourn more deeply than Mary? (2 Kg. 21, 10). Are we to imagine that Eos and Eurydice went further in their mother-love than Mary?[1] If Mary's compassion was less conspicuous, it was not because it was less felt. We must not fall into the trap of thinking of Mary as being above human emotion, different from the rest of us by reason of her immaculate conception and therefore aloof, remote from anxiety, withdrawn into herself and beyond the reach of sentiment. If Mary "pondered," keeping many things within her heart, it was not because she felt things less than we do but rather because she felt them more than we do. So great was her feeling that there could be no appropriate outlet. She *had* to ponder, and in pondering suffered more.

But for us, to whom appropriate outlets are constantly opening, the situation is different. Everywhere around us lie objects of our active supernatural compassion. The danger for us is to ponder and do nothing. Or even not to ponder. Idle compassion—the emotion inspired by grace but allowed to remain sterile—is worse than no compassion at all. It is the negation of virtue, a frustration of grace. What our Lord said to the Pharisees about following up the

[1] Eos was the mother of Memnon, who went to the help of his uncle, Priam, and was killed by Achilles; Eos pledged herself to her son's memory by being inconsolable for ever. Eurydice was Creon's wife and mother of Haemon, whose death she mourned by taking her own life. The story is given in the *Antigone*.

vision of truth has its application in the matter of following up the vision of suffering: "If you were blind, you would not be guilty. It is because you protest, We can see clearly, that you cannot be rid of your guilt" (Jn. 9, 41). The compassion which is locked up turns easily, like any other talent which is not traded with, to corruption. Such mean qualities as cynical indifference, imputation of blame, unwillingness to make allowances, preoccupation with one's own small difficulties to the exclusion of interest in the greater difficulties of other people, are often the effect of neglected compassion—a grace working in reverse.

If compassion is charity, then the expression of compassion will follow the order of charity. Its first object will be Christ in his Passion. By meditating upon the happenings of Holy Week, the soul comes to see into the Psalmist's reproach and to respond to its implication: "I looked for one [saith the Lord] that would grieve together with me, but there was none; and for one that would comfort me, and I found none" (Ps. 68, 21). Christ is not suffered to tread the winepress alone: the soul, together with Mary and the saints, volunteers companionship. "More than ever is our Lord thirsting for love," says St. Teresa of Lisieux, "and he finds, alas, few who surrender themselves to it." This is surely where even the least penitential among us can make his offering: all we have to do is to surrender, and grace supplies the rest. With the bride in the Canticle the soul can say, "Draw me," and God will see to it that the pursuit of his love is kept up . . . can say, "Show me," and God will see that there is no more wandering after the companions of yesterday (1; 3, 6). In the Passion we find our true attraction: the magnetism of love which cannot but invite compassion. "But my share in the Passion is so weak," cries the soul when the vision of Christ's infinite love begins to assume reality, "and in the face of such suffering there seems so little that I can do." True, there is little enough that anyone can do, but the word *passio* does not mean doing—it means suffering.

In bringing compassion to Christ, we bring compassion to the whole Christ—to his members as well as to his memory. The members of Christ are everywhere, wherever there is human suffering. We bandage his hands, we anoint his feet, we soothe the roughness of his skin. As the priest is the extension of Christ sacrificing, so the sufferer is the extension of Christ suffering. "But if it is their fault that they suffer?" It makes no difference. The fact they suffer is claim upon our compassion. We shall not be asked, "Did they deserve it?" but "Did they need it?" The neurotics, the failures, the misfits: all are sufferers, all are Christ.

Finally we must be compassionate even with ourselves; and perhaps this calls for the most difficult expression of the three. We must know our limitations and be patient with them. Never condoning weakness, never indulging in self-pity, we put up with ourselves in a spirit of supernatural compassion.

V: SIMON HELPS JESUS TO CARRY THE CROSS

5

Co-operation

THE CONSIDERATIONS to be submitted here will follow naturally upon the foregoing: compassion leading to participation. It is almost as if the intensity of Mary's sympathy was so great that, like a flame, it caught upon the material lying to hand and elicited from Simon of Cyrene the service which she herself would willingly have rendered. It is almost as if the words which she had spoken to the servants at the marriage feast of Cana were now addressed to Simon, telling him to do whatever he was told. Simon had to be *told* to carry the cross: he did not ask to carry it.

The cross not only resembles a sign-post but in a sense *is* a sign-post. It points two ways. In one direction it sanctifies, in another it condemns. It leads either to beatitude or to bitterness; it cannot leave us unaffected. This is only what you would expect if it is the significant instrument in the redemption of mankind. How could it do anything else if it is the means chosen by him who was "set for the fall and for the resurrection of many in Israel, and for a sign which shall be contradicted" (Lk. 2, 34)? No grace leaves us the same as before we received it: either we co-operate and are strengthened in character, or we reject the grace and are weakened. The greater the grace, the more is this evident. The responsibility of receiving the Blessed Sacrament worthily is such that not to receive it worthily is to "eat and drink damnation to himself, not discerning the body of the Lord" (1 Cor. 11, 29). Once the cross is seen to have a healing and strengthening character, an almost sacramental character, it may not be lightly laid down. Like the body of the Lord, it must be "discerned." To receive it unworthily is to reverse its possibility.

"But that is exactly the difficulty," it will be objected; "because one never does see that the cross is healing and strengthening—not one's own, anyway—and if one did, it would not be much of a cross." Such an objection is valid if the cross is taken up piecemeal, but surely it was our Lord's intention when he told us to take up our cross and follow him that we should take up the whole cross—all that we are called upon to suffer. Our Lord speaks about shouldering a burden and submitting to a yoke: the implication is that we take on the *business* of suffering. Had he restricted his meaning to the particular, he would have spoken about burdens—in the plural—and yokes. That the process involves taking up each new cross as it comes along is obvious —or there would be nothing to show for it that the doctrine was being followed—but there is no guarantee that this present cross which I am bearing now is going to feel, however well I bear it, sweet and light. The reverse is rather the case: the existing cross is felt to be worse than any that have been borne before. The determining factor is not the sense of healing and strength which is given by one affliction as compared with another; the determining factor is the act of faith and love. If any man will walk after Christ, let him pick up not only the cross which threatens at the moment but the cross which is composed of a sequence of crosses. A man is a disciple not only for the duration of an isolated suffering. Discipleship is a state, and to maintain that state the disciple must be ready to go on enduring. When the conditions of this discipleship are understood and fulfilled, the cross is seen as desirable. "I know that the cross is worthwhile. I may shrink from it—particularly in the actual experience of it—but I choose it. Finding Christ in it, I must find my happiness in it." The soul that can say this is learning about the lightness and sweetness of the yoke, about the health and strength which flows from it.

It was the experience of this knowledge, coming to him

in the physical act of bearing the weight of Christ's cross, that constituted the peculiar grace granted to Simon. In the ordinary way it is compassion, as has been suggested in the foregoing section, that leads to acts of service; here it was an act of service, and a compulsory one at that, which led to compassion. In the ordinary way it is attraction that leads to co-operation; here it was enforced co-operation that led to attraction. The sequence in Simon's case was a singular one: reluctant acceptance, actual contact with the wood, revelation, eager collaboration. Having made Christ's cross his own, Simon knew, inevitably, that the next thing to do was to extend this particular initiation into suffering so that it should embrace all suffering. Inevitably also came the knowledge that in doing this he would be effectively working with Christ for the redemption of souls. In the space of a few minutes, perhaps in a single instant, Simon became in the truest sense a "disciple"—a word which derives from the idea of learning and which denotes at the same time discipline.

How does all this affect us? The immediate lesson which the circumstance of Simon's cross-bearing teaches is that of receptivity. Had Simon closed his mind to the possibility of co-operation, nothing short of a miracle could have broken down the barrier. But because he came to the work disposed to see what lay behind it, he was given the light to see what lay behind it. So long as our minds are open to grace, we can confidently believe that grace will—even if it comes, as in Simon's case, from an unexpected quarter—make itself felt. To expect grace from one quarter only—as from the sacraments or devotions, or from this and that favourite work of mercy—is to limit to that particular area the distribution of a good which is designed to come to us from every direction. The saint is the man who, having no preconceived ideas about where his graces are most likely to be picked up, expects to find God's help in everything that happens to him. He is ready for the unlikely, he is open to the uncongenial contingency, he takes everything in his stride.

The second lesson to be learned from this instance of cross-bearing teaches us that when we identify ourselves with Christ we identify ourselves with his mission: we play a part in the act which intercedes, atones, and redeems. Our voluntary co-operation, in reproducing the work done by Christ, benefits the Church which is perpetuating Christ's interior and exterior act. Our sanctification is not our own affair alone; we are not detached units, each self-contained and self-determining. We belong to an organism in which the activity of its members affects, for good or ill, the health of the whole. From the doctrine of the mystical body, as also from the doctrine of the communion of saints, it follows that the pain of one member can do duty for the punishment of another—that vicarious suffering draws off poison with which others are infected.

So it is not only in the Mass that Christ's sufferings are represented; they are represented also in the sufferings of the Church. If the Church is its members, then the sufferings of Christ find constant renewal in the Church's members. The supreme vindication of this principle is to be seen in the Church's teaching with regard to martyrdom. Precisely because the martyr re-enacts the sacrifice of Christ, laying down his life for the love of God, he benefits the world for which Christ died. The martyr is not just an example of personal holiness and heroism—one man saving his own soul by violence—but rather he is a conductor of grace whose work for others in the Church has been effective because of his holiness and heroism. He has come so close to Christ's example that his sacrifice has won the glory of being united with Christ's in its effects as in its operation.

The sufferings which even the least of us endures are a reflection of martyrdom. They are a kind of mystical bloodletting. Through the wounds which life inflicts on us is poured the blood which, because it flows with that of Christ, speaks better than Abel's. The sacrifice of ourselves, made in the spirit of the New Law, cannot but be more pleasing to God than even the richest sacrifices of the Old. Should a

Christian be content merely to profit by the fruits of Christ's sacrifice, and not have any active share in the pain which constituted it? Should he not rather, with Simon of Cyrene, put his strength at Christ's disposal? Once a man is granted to see what the cross is all about, there would be little sense in his holding back. But we do hold back, and this is because we tend to be ruled not by sense—still less by love or by faith—but by fear.

VI: VERONICA MINISTERS TO JESUS

6

Generosity

"Everyone therefore that shall confess me before men, I will also confess him before my Father who is in heaven" (Mt. 10, 32). If the Church's martyrs were those whom our Lord had chiefly in mind when the words were spoken, Veronica must also have found a place in his thought. Hers was certainly an act which bore witness to Christ and to the truth of his gospel. It was public, it was heroic, it was spontaneous, it was prompt. As an example of complete and self-forgetting generosity, Veronica must have few equals in the history of the saints.

That Veronica expressed love is obvious; without love there would have been no impelling force. That she showed faith is hardly less obvious; without faith she would not have seen the Messias in the man condemned to die. That she expressed hope can be concluded from her love and faith; it must have been her hope in the promises made by Christ which denied the possibility of defeat. Where you have the three theological virtues working together to the soul's fullest capacity you get high sanctity.

Even in their ordinary exercise, as performed for instance by us who are not heroic, acts of faith, hope, and charity do not come easily. If they are costly in the measure that they are performed in the face of opposition, then the act performed by Veronica must qualify as of the highest merit. Assuming the tradition to be authentic which makes her the wife of a Roman official quartered in Jerusalem, Veronica would have known that another's reputation, as well as her own, was at stake. She would have heard in anticipation, during those brief moments when she was moving towards Christ, the voice of gossip which tomorrow would pass from one drawing-room to another in Jerusalem. To think that a woman in her position . . . and for a mere Jew . . . her unfortunate husband with his career to think of . . . they will have to go away, of course, and to some out-of-the-way garrison of the empire . . . not a very good example to the rest of us . . . if the man had been a Roman it might not have mattered quite so much . . . but a *Jew*. Veronica's conversion—whether dating from an earlier stage in our Lord's ministry or from this minute when she saw the procession coming along the street—was a grace for which she had to pay a price.

Then, too, there was the external act itself: the work of forcing a way through not only the crowd of hostile spectators but also the military guard. A rabble might, from sheer surprise, allow a reluctant passage to one who was seen to belong to Roman society, but for a trained squad of Roman soldiers to have yielded is matter of wonder. Veronica, her mind made up, was not going to be turned back for any reason. If the thought of disgrace had not deterred her, neither would now the thought of a mob's violence or of an army's discipline. Hers was evidently a spirit which could override revulsions and regulations alike.

What, moreover, if her charitable attentions were not wanted? What if our Lord were to show, when she finally got there, that he would rather she had not come? This was possible, after all. It might have interfered with his plan, it might have compromised him, it might have been as unwelcome to him as the proffered palliatives were to be unwelcome in a few hours' time. There was no guarantee that her pious intention would not be gently handed back to Veronica unfulfilled.

But what Veronica never doubted for an instant, or she would not have started off in the first place, was that even if her ministrations were not to be accepted, her gesture would certainly not be misunderstood. Others might misinterpret; Christ could not possibly. And it is this which gives us our cue in such works as we may suddenly feel inspired to perform. So long as the impulse is believed to have come from God, nothing can go wrong in the actual outcome. We can know for certain that the work which is inspired by God, provided it is not deflected in its motive, goes back again to God. The work may be judged unwise by others, may have no precedent, may cause a good deal of trouble, may even provide occasion for much imperfection on the side, may itself come to nothing, but so long as it is undertaken in charity and for the greater glory of God its course is set. Once we are launched on a project which has God as its term we have nothing to fear but our own weakness of resolve, nothing but our fatal tendency to deviate.

Often it is reflex considerations, rather than faulty first intentions, that spoil works of charity. Our Lord makes this clear in the parable of the two sons, where the original intention of one was as good as the original intention of the other was bad. It works both ways; the question turns on knowing one's own mind. The advantage of being able to change one's mind when the intention was a bad one to begin with is offset by the disadvantage of being able to stop short and turn round when the intention started out as a good one. Where Veronica knew her own mind and followed it, we for the most part follow many minds and so confuse our course.

It is not that the saints were inflexible, woodenly pursuing their goal between straight lines; it is rather that because their goal was unalterable they refused in their pursuit of it to be side-tracked. The distinction lies in the difference, not always to be easily seen, between obstinacy and fidelity. If we aspire to complete fidelity in this matter of responding to grace we must, while remaining flexible to further grace, be resolute in silencing the demands of self-interest. With the demands go excuses, and with the excuses go reassurances and congratulations. By that time the initial impulse has been stifled. If we aspire to obstinacy instead of fidelity we are in danger, not now of going back, but of going on without the moment-to-moment assistance of grace.

Applying the above to the incident in the Passion which we are considering, we can presume that if our Lord *had* preferred to go without Veronica's ministration, he would have given her the grace to alter the expression of her original intention. Her obedience to this new impulse would have been more meritorious than the obstinate fulfilment of her original purpose. Flexibility and fidelity, far from ruling one another out, go together. Obstinacy, far from being a sign of strength, is often the clearest sign of weakness and uncertainty.

If this smacks of excessive subtlety, there is all the more need to get back to the directness of Veronica's act. Virtue makes for simplicity rather than for complexity, and when the soul has counted the cost of a proposed action the best thing is to forget about everything save the business of remaining faithful to the immediate grace. In our projected acts of charity—acts which range from writing a letter of sympathy to rescuing a man from drowning—there are only two factors to be considered: God's will and our own co-operation. If it is God's will that I should do this thing, I shall be given the grace to do it in the way that he wants it done. If it is not God's will, and if I know that it is not, I may not do the thing. It is as straightforward as that. Where Veronica comes in to point the moral is in the matter of promptitude: hers was the hair-trigger response which showed the generosity of her heart.

The lesson of the sixth station is accordingly a very different one from that taught by the fifth. Where Simon was invited by the Holy Spirit to supernaturalize a necessity, Veronica was called upon to render a spontaneous service. Because she was in no way bound by the law of justice she is all the more to be reverenced for her act of supernatural

56

charity. If it was duty which drove her, it was the duty of living up to the challenge of love. Significant, too, was the nature of her reward: work done for Christ brings the imprint of Christ upon the work. When man makes Christ the first object of his endeavour, and keeps continuously without evasion to the programme proposed, he sees eventually in his undertaking the lineaments of Christ. Looking up he sees, with the disciples at the Transfiguration, only Jesus.

VII: JESUS FALLS THE SECOND TIME

7

Discouragement

PSYCHOLOGISTS TELL US that one of the chief evils of our age, an evil apparently less evident in earlier ages, is that of easy defeat. Be this as it may, most people who are honest with themselves would probably have to admit to indulging in despondency. They are fortunate if they have no worse to confess than despondency; there are many who labour under the weight of near-despair. Whether guilty of surrendering to the temptation or whether burdened with a sense of guilt which in fact is without foundation, a man can so reduce his spiritual vitality as virtually to close his soul to the operation of hope. When hope dies, there is very little chance for faith and charity.

It is a commonplace to observe that the saints were not those who never fell but that they were those who never gave in to their falls. It is less generally understood that the

saints felt just the same longing as we do for the excuse
to go on falling. The parable of the wheat and the cockle
should show us that the saints were not only as divided
against themselves interiorly as we are, but that they had
to go on struggling all their lives against the desire to let
the cockle have its way. A mistake we make is to think of
the saints as triumphing over temptation by the felt force
of ardent love. Some of them, certainly, experienced this
fire, but for the most of them it has been a question of
grinding out dry hard acts of faith and hope through
clenched teeth. The saints have had to fight every inch of
the way against discouragement, defeatism, and even despair.

How could it be otherwise? No virtue can be productive of good unless it comes up against the evil which is its
opposite. Courage is not courage until it has experienced
fear: courage is not the absence of fear but the sublimation
of fear. In the same way perseverance has to be tried by the
temptation to give up, by the sense of failure, by an inability
to feel the support of grace. The reason why Christ fell
repeatedly—one tradition would have it that he fell seven
times—is at least partly because we fall repeatedly and have
need of his example in recovering from our falls. The difference between his falls and ours is that where his were
because of weakness of the body, ours are because of weak-

ness of the will. The likeness between his and ours lies simply in the use which can be made of them.

Even if we do not reproduce the Passion in any other respect, we have the chance of reproducing it in persever-ance under exhaustion. If, as we have seen, the Passion is constantly being renewed in the members of Christ's mys-tical body, there must always be some aspect of Christ's suffering to which our own personal sufferings can show an affinity. If we are bearing witness to the same truth, oppos-ing the same evil, moving in the same direction, then the same means must be used by us as those which were used by Christ—namely, patience and endurance in the all but defeating experience of life. The effort which we make to regain the position lost by either circumstances or sin will reflect the effort made by Christ to return to the interrupted work of cross-bearing. Nothing of our experience need be wasted, not even our sinfulness.

So it would seem that the truly Christian man tran-scends discouragement only by accepting it. No man can pass beyond an obstacle except by facing it and rising above it. To go round an obstacle is not to overcome it but to evade it. Circumvention may be all right when travelling along a road, but it will not do when advancing towards God by the way of the cross. Of the three answers which are given to the problem of pain, it is only the Christian answer which is found to provide any lasting conviction. The Stoic approach, stifling complaint, can carry a man to heroism of a sort, but it does not supply him with a philosophy; it does not point to anything beyond a natural nobility to be developed in physical endurance. The Buddhist approach is more subtle than the Stoic: there is a Buddhist philosophy about pain, but it is a negative one. The suppression is applied not now to complaint, but to desire. Where the Stoic says, "I will not cry out for relief," the Buddhist says, "I will not cry out for anything." The Buddhist solution is that of emptiness; get rid of all desires and you will no longer expect relief, no longer be open to disappointment, no longer feel the weight of life.

Then comes the Christian ideal, which has nothing to do with negation and emptiness. Here is the invitation to take up the cross, here is St. Paul preaching Christ crucified and glorying in nothing save in the cross of Christ, here are the apostles going about glad to be accounted worthy to suffer for Christ. In the Christian dispensation happiness and sanctity are found in accepting the cross with Christ, bearing the cross with Christ, falling under the cross with Christ, and getting up under the cross with Christ, and going on in the knowledge that this is Christ's cross—discouragement.

A man cannot deny his discouragement any more than

he can deny his existence. It is part of his existence. All he can do is to deny himself the luxury of discouragement; he can mortify his tendency to self-pity. By becoming Christ-centred instead of self-centred, a man so reorientates his perceptions as no longer to see discouragement by the light of the world, or in its purely human context, but by the light of grace and in the setting of the Passion. If Christians lived out their lives in relation to the Passion—if their wills remained in proper harmony with God's will—they would be incapable of experiencing more than the first stab of disappointment, and would suffer only such pains as creation necessarily imposes. There would be no settled mood of disillusion, no dispirited pursuit of the second-best, no trailing of despaired purposes, no accepted exhaustions and wastes.

But since most people live in a lamentably distant re-lationship to Christ's Passion, inevitably there must result a lingering *malaise* in their lives which drains away their irreplaceable resources. Failing to see their place in the suffering body of Christ, they remain blind to the significance of their discouragements. What, after all, are the grounds for human discouragement but experience of inadequacy and loss? A man is discouraged either because he looks back at the past and sees a sequence of misfortunes which has shaped for him a mould of failure or because he looks into

63

the future and can see no security, happiness, prospects of success. His experience of life has given him these findings, so he feels, understandably, that life is insupportable. But if he knew more of Christ he would know that he had misinterpreted his experience, and that life is not at all insupportable. He would neither shy away from the thought of the past nor stand dismayed by the thought of the future. The immediate present would not daunt him either: he would know that it could be related, together with the failures that have been and the horrors that are in store, to the Passion.

This is not to say that deliverance from disillusion, discouragement, and despair can be effected by a mere trick of the mind—the knack of referring one's desolations automatically to God—but it is to say that in the gradual and painful conversion of the soul from self-centredness to God-centredness there will be a growing tendency towards confidence. No longer brought low by the sight of so much evil in oneself, in others, in the world, one rises by the slow deepening of detachment to the sight of a possible good in oneself, in others, in the world. The vision extends to a probable good, and then to a certain good. Together with this widening of a horizon which reveals the positive where before only the negative was expected goes the knowledge that the only good is God's good, and that it exists on earth—as those who receive the Word made flesh exist on earth—not of the will of man but of God.

In the measure that we allow our desolations to be transfigured by grace, so that they become part of Christ's desolation, do we bring at the most significant level comfort to others who are desolate. "If you wish men to weep," says Horace, "you must first weep yourself": if we weep for the right reason, we shall prevent others from weeping for the wrong one. If we unite our sorrows with those of Christ we not only sanctify our own souls, raising them above the discouragements of life, but also come to act as channels of grace to the souls of those for whom, like us, Christ fell and started up again on his way to Calvary.

VIII: THE WOMEN OF JERUSALEM WEEP FOR JESUS

8

Intention

IT IS A CURIOUS THING that while no human being can
go through a suffering in the same way as another human
being, all seem to want to communicate their experience to
others and to probe into that of others. We are created as
such close members of the human family that the instinct to
share extends to every emotion however painful, to every
experience however unsatisfying, inappropriate, risky. Even
those sentiments which we call secret are not so secret that
we do not want, on occasion, to air them. But when we at-
tempt to communicate the incommunicable we succeed
only in exposing the intimate.

It is this quality of wanting to go out to others, laying
bare ourselves and inviting a return of self-revelation, that
makes for the virtue of sympathy and for the vice of scan-
dal. Left at its purely natural level, the tendency may be

67

socially good, neutral, or bad, according to the tempera-
ments of the people involved. Put on the supernatural
level—informed by grace and exercised in Christ—the
tendency both represents a return to the original conception
of man and expresses a right relationship to Christ. Living
human creatures were designed to live as co-ordinating
units in an organism; baptized Christians live as cells in
the supernatural organism of Christ. The question to be
considered here is the education of the natural and human
so that it may play the part of charity and so become divine.

With original sin came division within the human per-
sonality, and new directions of self-realization. The forces
in man which had worked together for good, which had
reflected the unity of God in the unification of human
activity, began to seek each its own independence. (Mr.
Huxley describes it as the urge-to-separateness.) So from
the Fall onwards human beings have lived out of harmony
with God, with nature, and with themselves. The different
parts of man have laïd claim to rights of their own, looking
for satisfaction in food, sex, excitement, and the accumula-
tion of money instead of in the well-being which God had
offered. Inevitably man has come to misunderstand the
divine nature, the created order, and his own self. The
demands which are claimed by selfhood are artificially
stimulated by successive and increasingly materialist civili-

zations which know how to supply luxuries instead of principles.

With the Incarnation came a return to unity. Man might now find harmony in Christ. Christ assumed the urges-to-separateness and brought them into harmony within himself. By baptism, which is incorporation into Christ's body, man is enabled to rediscover his lost union, and can once again take his place in an organism which is greater than his own. But in spite of this unique grace, man can still assert his selfhood and contract out of the organism which alone can bring to him the peace which he wants. Just as our first parents damaged their capacity for charity when they fell from grace and lost their integrity (*integer, whole*), so we, by the misuse of the same freewill which was enjoyed by them, can waste the grace of charity and divide anew the unity of the supernatural life which has been restored to us in Christ.

Turning now to the eighth station, we can see our Lord dealing directly with this matter of separateness and unification. He is bringing back the diverted or separated emotions expressed by the women of Jerusalem to the unity of truth. He is telling them not to waste in an outpouring of purely natural pity an energy which may be directed towards its proper object, which is at the same time its source. Grace goes out from God and must be referred back again to him:

charity begins and ends in the unity of God, who is the alpha and the omega. Christ is explaining to the women that they and their children and their children's children are all one in the organism which is himself. If they weep, let them weep in true charity for one another and not merely because they happen to be witnessing a spectacle which moves them deeply. If they weep, let them weep because of sin, which separates them from their true centre, from each other, from themselves. If they weep, let them weep not *for* him but *with* him. Then there can be no waste, then can their sympathy make an effective contribution.

The only waste in life is leaving God out; the only missed opportunities are the occasions when we have stopped short at self instead of having gone on to God. So important a factor is suffering in our lives that Christ interrupts his journey to Calvary in order to purify the intention of the women's sympathy. At all costs God must not be left out of this; here is an opportunity of going on to God, and these holy women shall be given an insight not only into true compassion but into the Passion itself.

Without some such insight, the Christian would be incapable of practising penance. He would be able to go through the movements of penance, but his acts would lack supernatural value and merit: his acts would be routine acts, either purely neutral or, if performed in a spirit of vainglory, bad. Our Lord did not in the strict sense practise penance—because there could be nothing in his life which needed reparation—but he gave us in his Passion an *example* of penance: he took upon himself the sins of man and atoned for them in the most penitential way possible.

This brings us to the question of vicarious penance as performed by the followers of Christ. If the effects of personal suffering can be applied to other members of the mystical body, then the directing of the women's sympathy towards himself was at the same time a lesson taught by Christ in the transferability of merit. The Christian who truly enters into the Passion by co-operation in the searing experience of accepted suffering acts as a viaduct along which the graces of conversion and pardon are conveyed to the sinner. Acting with Christ and as Christ acts, the Christian saint puts at the disposal of all the merit of his labour. While there can obviously be no guarantee that the sufferings of one man, however holy, will be allocated to the redemption or sanctification of any one particular nominee, it can be confidently supposed that not only do the penances of one avail for the good of *all* but that the intention to help individuals by the process of vicarious expiation will be taken into account. Certainly there are many saints who have acted on this supposition, and in many instances the transference has been in the event confirmed. If when we pray for particular people we have the assurance that they are receiving grace from God, it is only reasonable to believe that the same thing happens when we suffer for them. It is not as though they were getting grace from *us:* they are getting it from God *through* us. The flex is not responsible for the light in the electric bulb; the radio has not composed the music which it transmits; the telephone lays no claim to possessing a human voice. We are not causes of one another's betterment; we are mere coefficients. The cause is God's grace, and the connection between one soul and another in the work of sanctification will depend upon how far one or the other, or both, can be found to live in Christ. Charity is the link as well as the channel, and where two human beings are living in charity—that is in God, for God is charity—the work of sanctification is mutual.

In conclusion, and in case the quality of a purely human pity is undervalued, it can be said that while the natural is not to be despised the supernatural is to be preferred. On the showing of the eighth station, the lesser is the ready disposition for the greater. Mourn we must, but our mourning should be for the evils that matter most. If this doctrine needed to be taught in the green wood, it needs all the more to be taught now in the dry. The evils inflicted upon the body of Christ have increased with the centuries, and there is less excuse today for mistaking the lessons of the Passion. If we claim to see, the guilt of our blindness will be the greater. The grace which opened the eyes of the women of Jerusalem is only waiting to be used, but perhaps we of this generation are too proud to weep. Too cynical? Too tired? Too indifferent? Too hard? It is surely significant that in our Lord's crisis a number of his men friends failed him; no woman failed him. Veronica, Mary of Cleophas, Mary Magdalen, the weeping women, even Pilate's wife, stood by him. The apostles, save for John, fled.

IX: JESUS FALLS THE THIRD TIME

9

Exhaustion

FOR MOST it is not the hard edge of the cross, tangible
and measurable, that crushes the spirit and calls for the
greatest endurance, but the weariness of going on under a
cross which seems to have no defined substance at all. Except at intervals when we are faced with making a decision
about it, the cross is hardly ever a known quantity. Granted
that it is the occasions when the issues are clear-cut that
condition the soul for cross-bearing, it is the dreary day-to-
day drag that constitutes the work at its most sanctifying.
The cross is not so much a given weight which presses on
our shoulders; it is rather that quality of suffering, un-
declared or only vaguely appreciated as a cross sent by God,
which comes up through the soles of the feet and spreads
exhaustion through every bone and muscle and nerve until

it reaches the head and turns even the mind to lassitude and disgust.

We always imagine that if we felt strong we would not mind having to carry the cross. But the whole point is that we should not feel strong. It is our weakness that very often is our chief cross. Given strength, the right mood, the sense of doing something big, the knowledge that we shall not have to keep this up for ever and that fairly soon the climax will be reached from which there must be a lessening of pressure—given, in other words, conditions of our own choosing—and any fool can manage it. Somewhere there has to be a weight about the cross, and most of the weight comes not from the thing itself, from the suffering imposed, but from the weakness which we feel in our powers of carrying it. The chief suffering lies not in coping with the cross so much as in *not* coping with the cross. It is in sinking under it a second and a third time, in the spirit of the *Septem Christi Casus,* that coping with the cross consists.

Confusion in this matter arises from what might be called the production fallacy. Provided the outward work produced is seen to tally with the original conception, it is judged to be a success; until the moment when it stands there, the visible achievement, it is judged to have no value. To take this view is to assess the quality of a work solely by its external effect; it is to leave out of account the merit of a work which may conform in every particular to the terms laid down as to the manner of its execution, but which, through an unforeseen arrangement of circumstances, fails in respect to the planned finish. Back again, it will be observed, at the question of frustration and failure. Say we spend years in working at a project which collapses before the end. At the moment of the collapse does some force suddenly travel backwards in time and vitiate the effort which has gone into the work? Not one of those years is changed by the failure; every effort is exactly as it was; each act of hope in the ultimate result remains unchanged. The only thing that has changed is the manner of the finish: the finish has been premature and not what was expected. The foregoing years were not charged with finish but with desire. The only thing that has got lost in the collapse is the one thing that apparently does not matter in God's sight—namely, the planned rounding-off. The wood of the sacrifice is perishable; the sacrifice itself is not.

This means that a work which is begun for the glory of God goes on giving glory to God *all the time*. It means that whatever the work looks like at the end, and even whatever it looks like if God wants it to be left off before the end, God's seal and blessing lies upon it. What can the Crucifixion have looked like to those who had expected our Lord

77

to bring the Roman occupation to an end? And yet it was from the cross that our Lord proclaimed his *consummatum est*. It did not look like it, but he had finished the work which his Father had given him to do. In what appeared to be perfect frustration was found the perfect finish. The only true completion to a work is the fulfilment of God's will, and this is done whenever God wills that our works be cut off short before their time. If we can say *Amen* to the apparent spoiling of our undertakings, we are putting the crowning touch to their achievement. The *Fiat* which expresses the saint's instinctive response to any happening in his life is, like the *Amen* which comes at the end of a prayer, a handing over to God of that which was inspired by him.

But even when we have had the sense to say *Amen,* accepting the cross with as good a grace as we can manage, the weariness of it all goes on as before. If this were not so we would be in the contradictory position of being able to get rid of our crosses by accepting them. Our Lord never said that those who took it up with him would find their cross melting away: he said that it would seem light to bear because their wills would be united with his. The cross is the cross whichever way you look at it, but if you look at it in the right way it is seen to be worth carrying.

Although it is true that the longer the journey the

greater the exhaustion, it must be remembered that against this can be balanced the increasing support of grace. Physically and nervously we may, in fact we do, grow more tired as we grow older under the weight of the cross. There is no glamour any more in the thought of continued endurance. We are bored with the theory of Christian suffering, we see no likeness between our own and the martyrs' fortitude, we wonder how it was that we ever felt the least attraction to the cross, we look back over a past which seems littered with rejected crosses, we conclude that perhaps the best thing to do is to think as little of that side of life as possible and to concentrate instead on prayer and charity, which evidently matter more. But this very sense of disillusion with self is part of our cross, and when it reaches the point where we almost despair of ever being able to reflect Christ crucified, where we seem to see ourselves weakly and heedlessly walking down the smooth broad way which leads to perdition, it becomes a very salutary cross indeed. It is teaching us some primary lessons in the love of God: it is teaching us humility and dependence on God. We may not see it as the cross, but often the most sanctifying crosses are those which we do not see. The cross is something which we see by, rather than something which we see. The longer we endure its pressure, the more deeply we come to appreciate the significance of suffering in others and the implications contained in the sufferings of Christ. It is this very vision which, however exhausted we grow in the process, makes the burden light and the yoke sweet.

In the case of our Lord's third fall we can count up a number of external factors which could have occasioned it. The Roman officer responsible for delivering Christ to the place of execution might have feared that the prisoner would die on the way, and so had tried to hurry the procession with orders which resulted in this final admission of spent strength. Or perhaps the soldiers themselves had got impatient of the business, and, anxious to come off duty for the leave which was due to them over the period of the Jewish holiday, had sought with added cruelties to spur their captive to a better pace. Or perhaps the going was more difficult the further from the city, and certainly the rising ground towards Calvary would have made a greater tax upon a burdened man. These are so many external circumstances and contingencies; what really accounted for Christ's fall was something inside Christ himself. It was something which stretched out to the Father's will, received it through the external setting of immediate causes, and referred it back again to the Father with infinite resignation and love.

In the case of our own collapses we are invited to follow, in our degree, the same process. There may be a hundred reasons, in the shape of concrete circumstances, why at any particular moment we had to give in. We have had to let go because of illness, because we have lacked support, because of promises broken, because of a change in superiors or because of new directions given to us under obedience. These are so many outward symbols used by God; they both point to and at the same time veil his will. They are signs which we can call material if we like, but which are meant to be interpreted spiritually. There is nothing outward that has not an inwardness of its own, and it is for us to discern by the light of grace what that inwardness denotes. The cross, and particularly the cross of failure with its attendant weariness, has an inwardness which denotes love.

X: JESUS IS STRIPPED OF HIS GARMENTS

10

Detachment

THERE IS ONE DETACHMENT which we bring about, and there is another which God brings about for us. The Christian who is trying to follow Christ on the way to Calvary does not confine his detachment to what he gives up; he thinks of detachment more from the point of view of what God takes. A religious man can become so deeply interested in the process of detaching himself from this and that—in drawing up his list of things to be shed—that he forgets what detachment is primarily for. So long as I say, "Lord, look with favour upon these renunciations which I am making for you," I have one eye on the generosity of my sacrifice. When I say, "Lord, I tend to cling so tenaciously to the things which I like that the best plan would be for you to detach me in your own way by taking whatever you want," I have my eyes on God. It is a fairly general rule that wherever there is less glamour there is more room for grace, and there is far less glamour in allowing God to take than in making self-chosen sacrifices.

But it is a doctrine which has to be properly understood. A man has no right to conclude that because he has nominally given to God a free hand, he can dispense himself from ever making a sacrifice. Far from providing a good excuse for indulgence, the principle of letting God take supposes an over-all declaration against indulgence. On the assumption that a measure of renunciation is recognized by the soul as absolutely necessary, it is suggested here that the grace of detachment comes more readily when the emphasis is on God's action than on one's own. Detachment is a grace but not necessarily a miracle. There has to be the will to detachment, and even the actual striving after detachment, before God grants the supernatural habit of detachment. We are inclined to make the mistake, when thinking about the relation between the gift and the use of the gift, of imagining that the reward comes first and that the virtue comes after—as one who would say, "I can wait for the grace of continence before I need try to be continent." While we have every reason to trust in grace rather than in any strength of our own, we have no reason to trust in grace as though it were magic.

Leaving aside the man whose laziness is supported by

superstition, who persuades himself that one day there will be a click in his mind and he will thenceforth be able to float along his way to God unencumbered by creatures, we can consider the alternative methods employed by two men who are seriously bent upon perfection. Both men hear Christ's summons to launch out into the deep. Both survey their respective crafts, and to each it must appear that his boat is overloaded for the task. One man says: "If I am heading for deep waters, I must take no risks. I shall have to throw overboard my cigarettes, my sherry, my spare clothes, my books, my pictures, my camera and my television-set. It is the price one has to pay, and after all one is doing it for God." The other man says: "I hate getting rid of anything. When it comes to choosing, I do not know what I am meant to keep and what I am meant to throw away. If I am heading for deep waters, I must take no risks. I dare not throw away something which may be necessary to me when the voyage gets under way. I dare not risk having to come back to pick up what I had stupidly judged to be ballast. I must put my confidence in God, and let him arrange the journey for me. It is he who has called me to do this thing, so I can believe that he will either wash overboard what is excessive weight or else give me the judgment to make these practical decisions as I go along." Where the first man is liable to alternate moods of dismay and vainglory, the second is made constantly aware of God's providence and of his own insufficiency. Where the first, devising an approach which may or may not be in the plan of God, limits the idea of renunciation to a particular area, the second gives unconditional scope to the divine action. The one looks at his boat more than at God, the other looks at God more than at his boat.

It was Christ's will that all his life he should do without luxury and even comfort. Unlike the foxes with their lairs and the birds with their nests, the son of man had nowhere to rest his head. He who owned all—to whom every inch owed rent—willed to have no place of his own. Detaching himself from what belonged to him, he lived for the love of the Father as a poor man. Not only did he choose to be without this and that, but he chose to let others take from him what they wanted. He submitted to being stripped of even those things which were for his necessary use. The tenth station shows us the extreme to which Christ's love of detachment took him. While many of those who aspire to the Christ-life will be deprived of their comforts, few will so nearly resemble Christ as to be deprived of their covering. But in spite of the gulf which exists between Christ's example in this matter of detachment and our own practice, there is occasion here for self-examination. Am I detached enough about dress, or do I set too much store by being comfortably or fashionably or expensively or strikingly clothed? Am I resentful when people take away my things and wear them? I must remember that while the lilies of the field are better dressed than Solomon, Christ had not the comfort of being as properly clothed as the plants which he had created.

If we are to be detached from soft living and all that pleases the senses, we are to be detached all the more from pleasures and possessions which touch us more closely. The pleasures of friendship, for example, are to be held in a loose grasp. A good friend is as legitimate a possession as a good suit, but the follower of Christ should be as ready to be stripped of the one as of the other. The man whose affections cause him to snatch at the response which he looks for in others, which cause him to cling to the time or the confidence or the exclusive love of another, has not understood the meaning of detachment. The more subtle the pleasure, the greater the need for detachment. At the moment when our Lord was allowing his clothes to be taken from him he was allowing his apostles to leave him. It is harder to be detached from one's followers than from almost anything else.

Detachment, if it is to be complete with the completeness of Christ's, must extend to one's good name. A man's reputation is as legitimate a good as can be had, but even here there can be occasions when the possessor must stand back and show a supernatural indifference towards it. In the approach to Calvary no prelude to the Crucifixion can be more apt than loss of standing. When the world turns against a man whom it once approved of, when the cry goes up that the hero had clay feet after all, the consummation cannot be far off. But a man has to be far advanced in detachment if he is to bear this trial with equanimity. If without dramatizing it in any way or indulging in the least self-pity, a man can watch the process of his own decline in public favour, and unite the experience to Christ's at the hands of the Jews, he is blessed indeed. Not many can bear the reversal of a confidence that has been placed in them.

Finally there is the detachment from oneself. A man may have renounced physical indulgence, may have risen above the intellectual delights of reading and the arts, may have surrendered his following of disciples, may have sacrificed his reputation for the love of God, but if he is to enjoy the grace of transforming union he has still to be stripped of his self-esteem. Layer after layer of self has to come off until he knows by the most intimate of all experiences—the experience of truth burning its way into the soul—that he is nothing and that God is all. He has to stand there and look on while the light of grace exposes one by one his evasions, part-playings; secret refuges, compensations, self-deceptions. Since there is room for self even in the disgust and humiliation which follow such a revelation—"he who despises himself," says Nietzsche, "nevertheless esteems himself as a despiser"—there must be a detachment once again. When full confidence in God has replaced the bitterness of self-knowledge, then can the soul be made ready for the final union. Not without reason do the earliest presentations of this station include in its title the mention of gall. That Christ at his stripping was handed the sourest of all drinks is a detail which implies much. The cup has always been the symbol of suffering, even when we think of it as the chalice of salvation, so we should not be surprised at finding in it vinegar as well as wine.

XI: JESUS IS NAILED TO THE CROSS

11

Perseverance

FROM AMONG THE MANY ASPECTS of the eleventh station which might be dwelt upon, only two are to be considered here: first the implication of finality contained in the idea of nailing, second the nature of the cross to which the modern Christian who is in earnest about his religion must expect to be nailed. That perseverance, or at least consistency of vision and thought, will come into the treatment of both aspects is obvious. Without the assumption of perseverance there would be little point in dealing with, or even practising, any virtue. Here it acts as a backdrop against which the twofold theme is played out on the platform of daily experience.

Few would deny, then, that one of the chief weaknesses of our time is the spirit of experimentalism. People try a thing, and if it does not immediately answer to their need

Director of Residence

they try something else; they do not want to be tied down. The desire to leave open a loop-hole of escape prompts the desire to escape, and life becomes a series of temporary ventures prematurely abandoned. Men and women are becoming increasingly reluctant to commit themselves: whether it is a question of a policy or a philosophy, a religious system or a career, the modern psyche claims the right to reverse its pledges at a moment's notice and to redirect itself along unexplored avenues of possibility.

So marriage becomes an adventure which is well worth trying; if the current partner turns out to be unsatisfactory, then the sensible thing to do is to make a change. A chosen occupation becomes a trial employment of faculties which are always on the look-out for something else. Where in other times a man looked forward in his undertakings to striking roots, the modern man looks forward to pulling them up. A man today will think little of changing his job, his house, his son's school, his religion, his political allegiance, his car and his wife—perhaps all in the one year. The present-day dislike of being pinned down shows itself unmistakably in the matter of modern entertainment: people prefer to come in and go out when they like, so choose the continuous performance of a film rather than the single performance of a play; they prefer to hear a concert which they can switch off to the one which commands a set attendance; they would rather eat and drink informally and standing up because to sit between two people at a dinner party would rule out the possibility of escape; they want to do their travelling by car because it avoids being committed to the times of trains; they read digests because they cannot face the ordeal of pursuing the whole book to the end. Always an unwillingness to go the whole way, to be bound to a course.

Against this we have Christ allowing himself to be nailed to the cross. He could have backed out, even then, but he did not. He was preaching a doctrine of stability, of completeness. The refusal to call the whole thing off may be called obstinacy by those whose purpose is flexible, but it represents an attitude much in evidence among the saints. If today people are slightly scornful of the stable man, charging him with a lack of imagination and initiative, it is because they are losing the sense of tradition—particularly of Christian tradition. The man who is stable will always be *useful* to his contemporaries in pretty well any society, but will he be held up by them as an example to be followed? Man tends to discredit the things he is bad at, and to canonize those which come easily to him. The urge to alter our lives every few years may well be hailed by future psychologists as a sign of health; steadfastness—is there already a faintly old-fashioned ring about the word?—will be at a discount. Fortunately there will always be the vows of religion to attract the world's attention to the essentially connected ideals of immolation and permanence—ideals implied particularly by the eleventh station of the cross.

Then comes the kind of cross to which the twentieth century is nailed. For having so long evaded the cross, padding it out with cotton wool, man is paying the penalty of being stretched upon a cross the existence of which the world does not recognize. Once the reality of sin is denied, the cross, which is the consequence of sin, has equally to be denied. Having done away with man's moral responsibility, the world quite logically does away with the idea of Christ's divine responsibility: the act of expiation becomes unnecessary, and the cross is made void.

But though the cross, as a Christian reality and in the terms of atonement, is repudiated, human suffering goes on. Pain is with us still, and though its existence is as freely admitted as ever—and indeed attended to as never before—it is attributed to causes unconnected with the Fall, is subjected to investigations unconnected with the Redemption, is given hope of relief unconnected with the Resurrection. Abandon the Christian concept of suffering as a mixture of punishment and opportunity, and you are reduced to proposing new explanations of human tendencies, new remedies for human ills. When acts which used to be expected to rouse a sense of guilt are accounted for by inherited compulsions, by immaturity, by environment, the sufferer who used to merit the reward of cross-bearing has to be content with being labelled an arrested affectionate, a socially starved, a victim of underprivilege, a case of abnormal mental sensitivity. Our troubles can be sympathized with because they relate to melancholy or fear or anxiety about money, but they may not be seen in the context of Christ's cross. We are nailed, inescapably, to a sacrificial wood which knows no sacrifice, to an altar the foundations of which are buried not in the common clay of our formation but in the unmined depths of our subconscious.

The trouble about tinkering with the subconscious is that, in getting down into it, all sorts of controls have to be released which are uncommonly difficult to regain when the investigations and adjustments are over. Nor is this only a matter affecting self-discipline; it is also a matter affecting faith. Consent given to the process which proposes the removal of compulsions and inhibitions may well prove to be a consent which removes other things besides. A case of taking off the head while taking off the hat, of throwing away the baby with the bath-water.

Morals, faith, and spirituality go together, and in order to recognize the cross for what it is, and still more to profit by it, there is need of all three. Determination to endure is not enough, and any system or science which leaves out of account any one part of the essential Christian ideal is bound to fall short of the truth. Certainly the man who is led to believe that God is a father-image, that hell is a fear-reflex, that the Church has arisen out of civilization's Oedipus complex, that a religious vocation is the result of an Electra projection, will not readily take to the idea that the cross of Christ is the instrument of man's salvation. It needs faith to see the sense of suffering, and it needs at least a measure of spirituality to accept it personally as something sanctifying.

To imagine that a man can reach the state of perfect well-being by a process of eliminating, one by one, the causes of his inner conflict is only less unlikely than to imagine that he can do so without God. Man is a centre of conflict, and the conflict is the cross. The more he tries to evade the conflict, the more he lays himself open to further conflicts and further crosses. In his preoccupation about ridding himself of the causes of conflict, he becomes subject to dread and doubt: he fears the outcome of the search. His dread of suffering will be his suffering, his feverish avoidance of the cross will be his cross—a cross which, as such, he refuses to acknowledge. Where to a Christian the element of fear is an accepted element of the cross, to the man who rationalizes every instinct from conscience onwards, fear is just another of nature's flaws—like loneliness and depression, jealousy and discouragement, and all the other horrors to which man is liable—and must be made good by the judicious study of the mind. Against all this business of rationalization we have the Passion telling us what is true suffering: pain and fear of more pain. The cross is the cross, and there is no substitute for it. Christ not only took it up for our sakes but for our sakes was nailed down upon it.

XII: JESUS DIES ON THE CROSS

12

Consummation

THE APPROACH TO CALVARY may be made by way of the Old Testament, by way of meditation on the Passion, by way of the Mass. But in the last analysis it is by way of experience. Until we have suffered something, however little, of Christ's last hours we do not know what pain, in the Christian scheme, is really for; nor do we know, until we have suffered with Christ, how bad we are at suffering. The Crucifixion not only opens our eyes to the gospel teaching on life as a whole and to the significance of the particular climax to which that teaching led up, but in its application to our own lives it throws into relief the standard of our religious conviction together with the generosity of our response. The Crucifixion, participated in, produces in us a twofold effect: Christ-knowledge and self-knowledge. It is by the knowledge of Christ that we come to the knowledge

of self: the sufferings which stop short at our own experience of them teach us far less than do the sufferings of Christ
which find their reflection in our experience. It is important
to see it in this order, otherwise we shall think of the Passion as no more than the projection of our own sufferings.
The Passion exists in its own right, in its own infinite right,
and whatever pain is ours must find its true place there.
The pains of a Christian are true and meritorious to the degree that they conform to the pattern set by Christ.

In the ordinary affairs of life we are bystanders, but on
Calvary we are bystanders no longer. For good or ill we
participate: we either let ourselves be caught up into Christ's
act or else refuse to be identified with it. Calvary represents
the peak in the Christian landscape: we are always either
coming up towards the summit or drawing away from it.
We cannot treat it as though it were not there. If we refuse
the invitation to join Christ in the final climax of his life, it
means that we have never faced ourselves, never grasped
the importance of sin, never understood about responsibility
and guilt. If we accept the invitation, we come to see how
inadequate we are, how corrupting sin is to us and what an
outrage it is to God, how deeply we are involved in our own
and other people's salvation or damnation.

Having once been granted to see, even to a small ex-
tent, into the closeness of the soul's relation to the Crucifix-

ion, we find that the sense of guilt is in danger of filling the whole horizon. Indeed the anguish which it causes is now the main constituent of the cross: it *is* the cross. But a worse cross is the one which is carried by those who deny a personal guilt, who are so afraid of self-criticism that they wrap themselves up in their pride. The agony of self-reproach is not so bitter as the false security of self-esteem. Better the memory of past infidelities which makes for a crown of thorns than the forgetfulness of past infidelity which makes for the crown of Lethe. Now is the time, while oppressed with the weight of unworthiness, to turn from the thought of self to the thought of God. If Christ on the cross has suffered so much for me, why should I despair? This act of his, to which my own sufferings have been united, was performed precisely to save me from what I fear. His Passion is my hope. The deeper the awareness of my sinfulness, the greater should be my confidence in his love. The thought of his mercy should eclipse even the thought of my guilt.

But this is not the end of it. The deepest human emotions are not as a rule related to our own troubles but to other people's. Certainly the nearer we get to the heart of Christ, the more we feel ourselves to be drawn into line with his own activity, which was that of loving and suffering for souls. When self-love frustrates and makes sad, the sadness is no deeper than the self which is loved. The sadness which

is caused by hurt done to the love we bear to others and to
God is infinitely deeper. It is as deep as charity. Can there be
any greater sorrow than that of having to stand by and
watch the seduction of the innocent and their subsequent
deterioration? To know that those whom we love in Christ
have rejected grace, have refused our help, and have set out
on a course which cannot but bring them unhappiness, is to
know suffering at its truest. Now again is the time—and
still more importantly, for the danger of despair is even
greater than before—when the gaze of the soul must be directed beyond the immediate occasion of the suffering to
the consummation of all suffering as seen in Christ. It is
now more than ever that we must count upon the force of
love crucified. The Crucifixion must be allowed not only to
do for us a work which we cannot do for ourselves but also
to do for those others whom we love a work which they cannot do for themselves, nor one which we can do for them.

The twelfth station should show us the power which
is possessed by love. It is stronger than sin. It expresses itself
in suffering, but it is stronger than suffering. It is stronger
than death and hate; nothing can stand up against it. This
is the essential lesson of the Crucifixion: the revelation of
absolute love. So much for the positive side of it—for the
part which Christ does and which we can help him to do—
but the tragedy is that on the negative side we can become

either so familiar with the symbols of Christ's suffering or so unfamiliar with the implications of our own that the Crucifixion is to us a matter of indifference. Like the soldiers at the foot of the cross we sit and watch—and see nothing.

Unwillingness to look at ourselves and admit our guilt extends to an unwillingness to look at Christ crucified and admit the price that is paid for our guilt. All that we see is a figure on a cross, and we have seen this so often before that we turn away and go on with our game of dice. It is not that we deny Christ but that we are no longer interested. We have other things to worry about—our crosses, for instance—and cannot give the time to studying Christ crucified. "It would be different," we tell ourselves, "if we did not happen to be overworked and bothered about money, if we had no family to think about, if we enjoyed better health and did not suffer from nerves, if there were not this ceaseless competition in the race of life. But as it is we cannot be expected to know Christ crucified or apply his life to ours." Against this we must believe that it is not a question of time or leisure in which to devote oneself to the occupation of love; it is a question of orientation. Nor, as has been suggested, is the secret of the thing to apply his life to ours so much as to apply our lives to his; our application is rewarded by the gift of himself so that we can say with

103

St. Paul, "I live, now not I, but Christ lives in me" (Gal. 2, 20), and go on to say, "I suffer now, not I, but Christ suffers in me." Just as in prayer we are not trying to bring down God's will to the level of our own but are trying to raise our own to his, so in suffering our effort should be rather to place our pains in his than to think of the process as bringing his into ours.

By a kind of spiritual *agnosia,* induced by the routine *sameness* of religious practice, we can come to miss the essential point of the mysteries presented for our belief. Taking all for granted in the sweep of faith, we allow our religious assent to stop short at the stage when true interior living should begin. The inwardness of the Passion remains to us unexplored. But the Passion, like the Church, must be something more in our lives than an outward symbol. While we may learn about the Passion through our outward senses—we can learn about it by no other way—we do not confine our understanding of it to the knowledge which comes out of books and sermons. The influence of the Passion upon our souls, as is that of the sacramental system and the liturgy, is psychosomatic—it is received physically and mentally, it is expressed physically and mentally. To the good Catholic—with his Holy Week book, his Sorrowful Mysteries of the Rosary, his crucifix and his stations—there is the tendency to let the Passion become a mere pageant, to let Calvary be a mere place of devotion, to let the cross be a mere sign. What is lacking to such a man's apprehension of Catholicism is the one thing which all these symbols of Catholicism denote and the one thing which Christ came on earth to give—namely, experience. Our Lord told his disciples to learn of him, not merely to look at him or stand in admiration of him. He was to draw men to himself, so that they might share *by experience* in his "lifting up."

XIII: JESUS IS TAKEN DOWN FROM THE CROSS

13

Aftermath

AN OPINION WAS CURRENT among the faithful of the early Church that only those who were martyrs could claim any real affinity to Christ in his death. To lay down one's life, physically, for one's brethren was considered to be the sole verification of Christ's "greater love than this no man hath," and so the only sure sign of heroic charity. But when martyrdom came to be less frequent, the Church began to develop St. Paul's idea of dying daily for Christ: martyrdom of the spirit was seen to be as sanctifying as martyrdom of the body. To bear, in one's life of prayer and penance, the marks of the Lord Jesus was just as much an ideal to be aspired to as that of suffering outwardly in the cause of truth. Indeed it might be considered an even higher ideal because of the greater faith required in its realization. With actual wounds to bear witness to his heroic charity, the

Christian has tangible evidence of his grace: he knows that what he is enduring must be acceptable to God and that the crowning reward of martyrdom lies only just round the corner. The man who is enduring his mystical martyrdom, on the other hand, is given no assurance whatever that his hardships are pleasing to God. Therein, precisely, lies his trial.

Thus death to self came to be valued as the main thing, death to the body being only one of its forms. Thus mortification came to be valued as a lifelong exercise, the mortal act of dying being only its closing movement. Thus the disposition of the will came to be valued as the qualifying factor, the actual disposal of life being a contingency to be prepared for and prayed about. Then, when we look back from the development of Christian spirituality to the source of Christianity, we see the principle confirmed: the emphasis given in the discourses of our Lord is upon life rather than upon death. Death to self must go on during life; it is not something brought about at a single stroke. We are led with Christ to the slaughter, we are put to death all day long.

This will mean that our mortification will be found in anticlimax just as much as in climax, in reaction just as much as in action. It is a matter of common experience that souls who have braced themselves to meet a particular trial, who have endured the suffering with courage while the crisis lasted, go suddenly to bits in the period immediately following. The kind of warfare upon which we are engaged is a continual one, and we can never afford the rest from struggle which in other kinds of strife might be expected as a sequel to success. Our participation in the Passion covers the whole of our lives; it is not for the moments of conflict only. Indeed our lives as Christians can be seen as a succession of deaths, each one followed by a period of its own particular mortification. We are taken down from the cross, but we have still a way to go before we can enjoy the full benefit of the Resurrection in the possession of eternal rest. The addition of the two concluding stations to the one which commemorates the last and most significant of Christ's acts on earth is designed to show us that while we are meant to unite ourselves with him in his death by crucifixion, we are meant also to remain united to him in his death at deposition.

Our example here is Mary. For her the work of suffering went on beyond the twelfth station. It has been suggested by theologians that since her capacity for love was ever expanding, the contribution made by Mary to her Son's purpose was greater after his death than before. Certainly her sufferings cannot have been less intense when she received his body from the cross than when she saw him hanging on it. The whole of Mary went out to the whole of Christ, dead or living. There is this also to be considered about Mary's compassion, that not only did she suffer on one particular day for one particular Person, but that she suffered all her days for all who belonged to her Son's mystical body. We are now at this moment enjoying graces merited for us by Mary's sympathy as expressed at the taking down of Christ's dead body from the cross. Mary, having accepted the responsibility of being mother to mankind, bears still the weight of Christ's mystical body. The concerns of the Church are her concerns, the Church's sufferings were given to her from the cross and she has never ceased to bear them. Individually and collectively we are able to count upon Mary's help before, during, and after whatever trials are ours.

Hitherto we have been considering the need on the part of the individual to look to the Passion for a solution to his problem of suffering; now for a moment we can consider the same need to be met by the same solution but on the part of the Church as a whole. A glance at Christ's mystical body as it is living on earth today shows us a picture of suffering among his members which must be unique in history since the time of the early persecutions. Within the decade following the second World War—itself hailed as the re-crucifixion of Christ[1]—Christians belonging to six-teen nations have fallen under Communist rule, and so for the most part have been deprived of the free use of the sacraments and of the Christian education of their children. In some of these countries—particularly in China, Korea, Poland, Hungary, Yugoslavia—the Church has been ac-tively persecuted. Wherever there is eviction, slavery, spolia-tion, martyrdom, or the suppression of the Mass and the sacraments, there is a continuation of the Passion. The crisis of Calvary is re-enacted, and we sit and watch. The serious-ness of our present international and religious situation is measured by our ignorance of it: we know that there is something wrong, but we do not know what is wrong. "And anyway," we say, "I cannot do anything about it." "And anyway," we say, "an atom bomb or a hydrogen bomb or some other kind of bomb will blow the whole thing to bits before long, so what is the good?" "And any-way," we say, "it will be the same for everyone else."

A more serious menace to the Church's life than even atheistic Communism is apathetic Catholicism. The real enemy is not the persecutor from without but the spineless

[1] Caryll Houselander, *This War Is the Passion* (New York and London, Sheed & Ward, 1941); reprinted 1947 as *The Comforting of Christ*.

Catholic within. "Satan owes his strength," it was pronounced at the Beatification of St. Joan of Arc, "to the easygoing weakness of Catholics." This is Christ's body that has become weak. We have become so accustomed to seeing Christ's body re-crucified in various parts of the world that we have rationalized his presence in the world. We have become so used to seeing sin everywhere that we have rationalized that too. "The greatest sin of our generation," said Pope Pius XII, "is that it has lost the sense of sin." As in the individual soul's relationship to God, so in the world's relationship to God: the outward circumstance is made to account for the evil, and the inevitable bent of man's nature absolves him from responsibility.

Nor is the emergency over. "The next twenty years of the Church's life," said Pope Pius XII in January 1946, "will have no parallel in history." In the following year he said that "men must prepare themselves for suffering such as humanity has never seen before." From *Evangelii praecones* of 1951 come these words: "The human race is involved in a supreme crisis which will issue in either its salvation by Christ or its utter destruction." In 1955 the Pope's warning is repeated: "We try not to hide from our own eyes, nor from the eyes of those who listen to us, the spectacle of a sky covered with clouds. The prospect is enough to make it look as though an overcast twilight were approaching, almost as though night were about to come down upon the whole world." The faithful's indifference to the utterances of Christ's Vicar is confirmation of what has been suggested above. How many Catholics study the encyclicals or know anything about the Church's social programmes? No wonder the darkness of Calvary is repeated over Christendom, hiding his body even from those who should know where to look for it.

This is the body mourned over by Mary at the thirteenth station of the cross. But there is one significant difference between the original deposition and the present: Mary kept silent on Calvary; today wherever she reveals herself, she speaks. After what she said at Cana, Mary is not quoted as saying anything more during her lifetime. Perhaps it is because her last recorded words have not been heeded that Mary comes again to insist that whatever her Son tells us we must do.

113

XIV: JESUS IS PLACED IN THE TOMB

14

Waiting

WHILE IT WOULD BE A MISTAKE to think of man's life
as a drawn-out agony, there would be nothing wrong in
thinking of it as reflecting the sequence of Good Friday,
Holy Saturday, Easter Sunday. Between the pain and death
of Good Friday and the triumphant joy of Easter there is
the long still period in the tomb. No phase of our Lord's life
and no aspect of his death may be neglected: the time when
his body remained in the darkness is not so much an interval
which separates as a link which joins. If the fourteenth station were just an afterthought, it would have dropped off
long ago. Certainly there is much to be learned from it—if
only because for most of us the work of waiting has more
of a place in our lives than that of either ministering, com-
passionating, or dying to self. The whole of man's life is a

waiting, and if we learn how to do that right we have found the answer to the problem of human existence.

Consciousness of being delayed on the way to eternal life differs in people according to temperament and grace. Even in the individual it is stronger at some times than at others. But for some the homesickness for eternity is an abiding reality, which, in its alternations of joyous hope and lonely longing, is all the time preparing them for the blissful moment of death. To those who look forward in this way, the act of waiting may sometimes occasion more natural impatience than it does supernatural love. When this happens, the soul's desire will have to be redirected towards the essential and away from the superficial. The superficial is shown up where there is a greater interest in the immediate means, which is death, than in the end, which is God.

Wherever the emphasis is on the detail and not on the whole there is risk of neurosis: death, either the love of it or the dread of it, can become an obsession. If fear of death can be a severe trial, so also can the love of it. Of the two, the shrinking is more straightforward than the longing: the one is frankly natural and instinctive, the other is either a work of grace or a subtle temptation. It is important to get one's attitude right as regards death because so much of one's attitude towards life depends on it. Life, the significant, can be coloured by death, the accident. It is one of the few instances of having to insure the primary by attending to the secondary. Death is secondary, but once it has been attended to, the soul sees life—with all its sufferings, happiness, loves, contradictions—in perspective. Death is seen *as* secondary, and no longer as the final goal.

The man who inordinately desires death cannot, however firmly he acknowledges the primacy of life, give a perfect service to God on earth. Nor can he find happiness. Life in this world, instead of being just a bore as it is to most moderately unhappy people, will be to him a pain. He will be lonely with the loneliness of exile. It will be hard for him to settle. He will be only half alive, for his desire is elsewhere. The man, on the other hand, who has made up his mind about death, whether to face it if he fears it or to endure delay if he hungers for it, is in a position to live for God and die for God. He will be able to say with Edith Stein as she was halted for a few minutes on her way to the gas-chambers of Germany: "We are travelling towards the east, towards the dawn."

To await the dawn of the Resurrection while struggling here with life and death is bound to involve darkness. While "the night was in the midst of her course" (Wis. 18, 14) came Christ to redeem the world, and again out of the darkness of night he rises from the dead. And so it must be

117

for man: through the darkness and the cloud he must look for the light of the world. Always waiting, in darkness more or less, feeling unsure and unsafe yet always trusting—such is the life on earth of the follower of Christ. The Christian virtues are evidently those which, like a plant called the marvel of Peru, grow mostly in the dark. Here anyway, in the sealed tomb where the body of Christ has been laid, do we see the fulfilment of the words already quoted about the ways of the just man being shut up with square stones (Lam. 3, 9). If stones, shutting out the light, blocked the entry to Christ's sepulchre, then those who claim to follow Christ should have nothing to complain about in the darkness which surrounds them and the blocking of their desires.

If we have mentioned the Christian virtues as flourishing in opposition—in what might be taken to be an alien element but which in fact is the element most conducive to growth—we should note that even pagan writers admit the value of perseverance in darkness and of endeavours unrealized. Classical legend gives instances of heroes who have gained spiritual stature precisely in the pursuit of quests which were doomed to failure from the start. While the adventures of Ulysses were told by Homer in verse, the odyssey which each man makes for himself is all the more heroic because so hideously prosaic. The lives which could

118

not be written, let alone written in the poetic form, are often the most painful—and for that reason the nearest to Christ. We go wandering through life, muddling up our crosses and slopping through our pleasures, and have nothing to show for it before God. But if all along, in spite of having fallen so often for temptation, we have wanted virtue rather than vice, God rather than self, charity rather than uncharity, we shall be nearer to God at the end than when we began. We may feel no nearer than when we first started out on our voyage of discovery, and probably we feel farther away because we see in retrospect the risks we have run and the wrecks we have been responsible for; yet by the time we die we shall be the wiser for our odyssey. Wiser because more humble; wiser because we have suffered and experienced; wiser because we have been drawing nearer to Wisdom itself.

Once while meditating at this fourteenth station a man in whom the desire for eternity was mixed with a strong dislike of living prayed earnestly that the day of his release might be hastened. In the meantime (he said) he would be ready enough to endure the cross and the darkness; it was this endless waiting (he told God) which he could not face. Before he knelt down for the *Pater, Ave,* and *Gloria,* he was given interiorly to understand that the waiting *was* the darkness and the cross. But it takes faith to see the cross

119

in the dark—particularly in the not so obviously dark night of waiting. It takes faith to see the point of that day and night in the tomb. Reason would suggest that with all his gifts it was a waste of time for Christ to be dead when he could have been living. He was the lord of life; he had only to say the word, and he need never have seen death at all.

Always we are being driven back upon the truth that the seed must die if it is to live, that a man must lose his life if he is to find it. It takes faith to see the fruit of futility. So important in the soul's development is suffering that, like prayer, it must mostly be exercised in the dark. If we could see our sufferings clearly we would want to handle them ourselves—just as if we could see our prayer clearly we would want to handle it ourselves—so God has to throw over them, over our sufferings and prayers alike, the covering of night. And in the night we think of them only as rubbish, as waste material to be thrown away. But none of it is thrown away. God fortunately sees to that.

As well as darkness, in the tomb was silence. In the work of waiting, silence and darkness seem to go together. They heralded the act of creation, so it is not surprising that they should accompany the act of redemption. Before the Nativity there was silence with the darkness: "While all things were in quiet silence . . . thy almighty word leapt down" (Wis. 18; 14, 15). Silence plays its part with darkness before the Resurrection. "It is good to wait with silence," says Jeremias, "for the salvation of God" (Lam. 3, 26).

When we come to the deepest of our sufferings we find we have nothing to say. God must know what we feel and man cannot—so why speak? For many the inability to sort out and articulate is a silent suffering; for others the desire to cry out is stunned to silence by the suffering itself. Either way it is the Passion, not smothering or crushing but rather stilling and making ready. In silence and hope we spend our vigil till the light of the Resurrection breaks through the dark.

Epilogue

THE EPILOGUE to the Way of the Cross is simply the sequence of Resurrection, Ascension, Pentecost. So what follows is more in the nature of a postscript than of a condensed continuation. In any narrative, whether it is a history or a mystery story, once we know what happened next we can go back and develop our theory. In the present instance the theory is that to understand the stations of the cross in the light thrown on them by the risen Christ is to understand in outline the pattern of Christian life. This is not to claim that the whole of faith and morals is contained in a knowledge of what happened between the condemnation and the sealing of the tomb; it is merely suggested that for those who work out its implications the history of the Passion, Crucifixion, and Resurrection provides a comprehensive scheme of Christian thinking and an adequate code of Christian action. If one were called upon to explain Christianity to savages, for example, one would not go far wrong in making this theme the basis of one's instructions. The Church's dogmas, sacraments, commandments, liturgy and tradition could be left until after the idea of a God who was born into the world to suffer with the rest of us and who rose again to give us proof and hope had been assimilated. There is nothing like the desert-island test to discover what our basic principles are and how we would set about their practice.

A question now arises. If the subject-matter under review is enough to save souls and even lead them to perfection, why does it not more generally do so? You would have thought that so accessible a design for praying, thinking, and acting would be more widely successful. We all have to suffer: there in front of us stands the Passion: we know what to do next. Why are we not all saints? Why does the formula not work? Many answers might be given to this, but a threefold argument, with each of its aspects relating to the other two, may be taken to cover them all.

In the first place Passion-Death-Resurrection is not a formula. Here are involved three separate mysteries which are essentially linked together and in which man finds salvation. They are mysteries, not magic. To approach them as though taken together they formed a panacea against

123

which our fallen tendencies could make no further stand is to approach in superstition and not in faith. There is all the difference between faith and fetishism. The danger among religious people who are not religious enough is to fasten on a doctrine, wrench it from its context, and apply it as if it were a poultice. Errors of this kind can be caused by a wrong understanding of the function of symbolism: the emblem can come to mean more than the truth which it represents. Symbolism, by a process of abstraction and concentration, is meant to focus the attention upon the meaning of a particular doctrine, mystery, act or event: it is not meant to take the place of it. So if the Passion fails to produce among Christians the sanctity which might be expected, it is not the Passion's fault. It is the fault of the Christian who gets no further than the instruments of the Passion, who sees only the scenes of the Passion, who gives nothing in return to the Passion but a superficial devotion to its symbols. The Passion is a grace to the soul, and if the soul is to benefit there must be a response at the same level: it means giving. Christ is the central figure, giving out and drawing in. The Passion is not Christ's sacrifice only; it is ours as well.

Arising out of this there is the second point in the argument accounting for the Christian's failure to make good the promises of the cross. The explanation is surely this, that he never truly lives the cross-bearing life. At intervals he meets the Passion, but it does not become part of him, nor does he become part of it. The Passion remains always on the perimeter of his existence—to be referred to in moments of crisis but not as something of second nature. Without the will to live in the Passion, the Christian can go a step further and find himself without the will to live in Christ at all. By rejecting the Passion's appeal for co-operation, the Christian not only impoverishes his own spiritual life but at the same time reduces the vitality of the other cells in Christ's mystical body. Spiritual deficiency, *anorexia* of the soul, is a disease which is very catching.

Living in Christ by baptism only, and not by active co-operation, the soul will find it no easy matter to keep in a state of grace. Where the Passion is held at a safe distance there is no longer a sensitiveness to sin. Just as the muscles instinctively tighten at the threat of a blow, and the eye instinctively blinks when sand is blowing about, so the man who is trying to deepen his understanding of the Passion is instinctively aware of the presence of evil. If he lets go of the Passion, temptation finds him with his defences slack. At the first movement of the Passion, our Lord told his

125

disciples what to do if they wanted to avoid entering into temptation. But they did not do it, and their descendants have not done it either.

For us who know every detail of the Passion there is not the excuse which lets out those less favoured than ourselves. There is always that awful reproach of Christ's to those who claim to be religious men: "If you were blind, you should not have sin. But now you say 'We see,' your sin remains" (Jn. 9, 41). Is it that we *have* seen, and have forgotten? Or is it that we have never really looked? It is interesting in this connection to note that immediately after recording the words just quoted, St. John goes on to give the parable of the good shepherd. Christ is known by his own, by those who share the kind of life which he leads, but not by the hirelings. The hirelings, by classing themselves among Christ's own while not prepared to know him on his conditions, are spoiling their chances. At the first emergency they are off.

What the Passion asks of us, then, is that conversion of heart and mind which is ready to go deeply into the matter and which is ready to be committed. Lacking such a psychological revision—the Greeks gave it the name of *metanoia*—there can be no true appreciation. Half-blind, we shall just go on seeing half-truth. And our sin, at least half of it, will remain. The way to clarity of vision, wholeness of vision, is open to us. No sooner had Christ finished speaking about the shepherd and the different kinds of sheep than he began to speak of laying down his life and taking it up again (Jn. 10; 17, 18). The Passion, Death, and Resurrection: it is knowledge of these mysteries—and a knowledge which is not academic merely—that gives us sight.

Lastly there is need, in our approach to the Passion, of completeness. If the *metanoia* is to work, it must not only reside in, and be affected by, the whole mind but must extend to the whole truth. While the finite intelligence is incapable of apprehending all truth, it is certainly capable of bowing before all truth. Our failure lies not in refusing to acknowledge truth where we see it but in refusing to bow before it—that is, to pay practical homage to it in our lives. The whole and only real tragedy in the Christian life is to let the incarnation-redemption truth be of no avail.

A Church which is catholic is also comprehensive, and just as fidelity all along the line is productive of sanctity, so the response which is selective is restrictive of sanctity. Our thesis is that a whole surrender to Christ's Passion gives us an understanding of the whole of life, and that an appreciation of part of Christ's Passion gives us only a devotion. If you asked an actor what the play was like in which he was acting, and he replied, "I don't know, I haven't read it; when I have said my lines I put on my hat and go home," you would judge that the richness of his profession had escaped him. If you asked a painter's assistant who was engaged in painting murals whether he admired the artist's composition, and he replied, "I'm not interested in compositions; I'm interested in colours; I see to the blues and greens," you would judge that though he might be excellent at his job, the man should widen his horizon. In life—all life, but particularly the spiritual life—we need to look at the design as well as at the detail: at the purpose of the Passion, not only at the particular setting. We see this only when we look with the eyes of the soul wide-open. "You shall seek me: and you shall find me," says the Lord through the prophet Jeremias, "when you shall seek me with all your heart" (Jer. 29, 13). The Passion is not only something we see more *of,* the more we contemplate it; it is something we see more *by.* It is not something which reminds us more of ourselves, the more we contemplate it; it is something which reminds us more of our relation to others in Christ. It is not even something which tells us more about the physical side of it than what we know already out of books; it is something which opens to us the mind of Christ.

DATE DUE

AP 21 71		
AP 3 72		
GAYLORD		PRINTED IN U.S.A.

www.ingramcontent.com/pod-product-compliance
Lightning Source LLC
LaVergne TN
LVHW012126070325
805405LV00001B/283